Dream
Cabinet

Dream Cabinet

Ann Fisher-Wirth

*For Chana —
with many thanks
and warm affection,
Ann*

WingsPress

San Antonio, Texas
2012

February 2012

Dream Cabinet © 2012 by Wings Press for Ann Fisher-Wirth

Cover photograph: "Hollandale Slough" by Maude Schuyler Clay
Used by permission.

First Wings Press Edition

Print edition ISBN: 978-0-916727-93-2
Ebook editions:
ePub ISBN: 978-1-60940-225-9
Kindle ISBN: 978-1-60940-226-6
Library PDF ISBN: 978-1-60940-227-3

Wings Press
627 E. Guenther
San Antonio, Texas 78210
Phone/fax: (210) 271-7805

On-line catalogue and ordering:www.wingspress.com
All Wings Press titles are distributed to the trade by
Independent Publishers Group • www.ipgbook.com

Library of Congress Cataloging in Publication Data:

Fisher-Wirth, Ann W.
  Dream cabinet / Ann Fisher-Wirth. -- 1st Wings Press ed.
    p. cm.
  Includes bibliographical references.
    ISBN 978-0-916727-93-2 (pbk., printed ed. : alk. paper) -- ISBN 978-1-
60940-225-9 (epub ebook) -- ISBN 978-1-60940-226-6 (kindle ebook) --
ISBN 978-1-60940-227-3 (library pdf ebook)
  I. Title.
  PS3606.I79D74 2012
  811'.6--dc23
                        2011048304

Contents

For my family

Slow Rain, October

Minds like beds always made up
　　　　　—William Carlos Williams

Oh to dive into an unmade bed and sleep,
and sleep, and sleep. The room is shadowy,
covers piled in a heap with pillows
still scrunched up, one halfway down the mattress
for my knees, two near the wall for our heads.
Outside, leaves draw closer, and as night
seeps from the forest, spills over the wet

back yard, climbs the stairs to the deck,
spreads its cloak and foggy stars across the window,
I die now for a little while: even the family photos
in the Welsh cabinet by the bed are strange to me—
parents marrying, parents aging, children small,
children grown, husband and wife
(that's I) embracing—sixty years of family.

Sweetness of not making the bed today,
not making the body today, not making
the life today. The pilot light flickers in the heater,
source of warmth in this old beadboard house
with its drafts and cracks and currents.
Three white roses on the Welsh cabinet
open further, ripen, slacken, begin to bruise.

I.

1982. Sophocles' *Philoctetes* in Athens

Athens, July, so hot we slept much of the day
and wandered the city all night, drank tea

in Syntagma Square writing postcards
to our families, loitered listening

to sidewalk guitar at 2 a.m. in the Plaka,
napped as the sun rose on stone benches

in the ancient agora. We prided ourselves
we were not like the tourists, cameras slung

around their necks, who clambered chattering
from tour buses and trudged in clumps

to the Parthenon as we rose from our bench,
sneaked another joint, deliquesced off to bed.

You said, *We don't need pictures, we will let
the moments pass.* I said, *We will walk these streets*

forever. Oh we were young and arrogant.
Our last day in Athens I lay on the bed, you sat

on the straight gray chair, over your shoulder
soft light from the afternoon rooftops slanted

into our sparse off-the-street-discovered hotel room.
You were reading Sophocles' *Philoctetes,*

holding your book up to the window, lips moving,
body swaying, black hair in a cloud around your face,

and for the first time ever you frightened me.
When I speak of that time my tongue

grows thick and I think of the family I broke
to be with you; years later my daughter told me

her father said to her, *You will have to be
the mommy now.* And what of Philoctetes,

exiled on Lemnos by the Greeks because of
the stench of his suppurating wound?

Some say his wound made him stronger,
gave him creative power. Or did it just hurt

forever? Twilight gathered in the room
as you read on, swaying, lost inside that suffering.

1972. Disorder and Early Sorrow

How attentively can she read Thomas Mann
if that is all she is doing for the summer
while her husband is in Ghana and her marriage
is failing? How slowly can she eat two pieces
of buttered toast cut up with two hard-boiled eggs,
can she make it take an hour? Add a nectarine,
add making the bed, taking a bath, washing
her hair, there's her morning. Too hot
and smoggy to go anywhere, besides she doesn't drive,
besides her only two friends are out of town.

She sits in the chair beneath the lemon tree
in her parched and rocky California garden,
practically lip-reading she's moving so slowly
and carefully through *Buddenbrooks*,
Death in Venice, Magic Mountain, Doctor Faustus.
She reads Mann on Nietzsche, Mann on Freud,
Mann on Goethe, Mann on Shakespeare,
she thinks she'll tackle *Joseph and His Brothers.*
Why Mann? Because she wants to be expert
on something? Because it comforts her,
all this heaviness and melancholy—overripe
strawberries and chlorotic teeth, disorder
and early sorrow? Then till four in the morning
she moves around the house—doing what, exactly?
There's no music, she doesn't watch TV.
Does she clean? Wash clothes?

Cigarettes keep her going. She's not entirely
kidding when she comments to herself
that Mystic Mints are a conduit
toward enlightenment. She gets a letter
from her husband and thinks she loves him after all.
He tells her he got stoned, fell down a five-foot
hole in the road, tells her his camera
and the dress he bought her were stolen.
She writes him back, pages, with honeyed words.
He's a good guy, a trip leader, building a clinic
with students. But it's not going to work,
she knows it. If only she could be different.

One night she sits till dawn, the door is open,
crickets clamor in the lemon tree,
she is not reading now, just waiting.

✓ **Answers I Did Not Give
to the Annulment Questionnaire**

*(After 14 years of marriage, 22 years of divorce, my ex-husband
wants an annulment)*

*annul: to bring to nothing; to do away with; make of no effect;
invalidate; make null and void; cancel. Ad, to + nullum, nothing,
neut. of nullus, none. Syn. see abolish.*

See me, a girl
                        school dress

        fog
                        organdy curtains

now I bite the polish
                        that has strayed beyond my nails

ignoring my mother, keeping her company

                soon I'll be told to set the table
                                every night
                        unpack the food
                                dry the dishes
                        clean my room

                                        But this

is the not-yet

About a boy

    I wanted so much
    we married

———

A boy and girl

    entering the restaurant at Manka's Czech Inn
    at Inverness by the water where they
    could afford two nights' honeymoon, blushing,
    dressed to the teeth,
    scraping every bit of flesh from their grapefruit

———

A girl by the freezing altar vowing
this would be her husband for always,
this would be her Church for always,
even if she was wrong, even if it came
to doors slammed and her locked outside
in the rain, and the children crying

———

So crazy
    about being his wife

        insisted on ironing his boxers

            Too poor to buy a bed,
            we jammed twin beds side by side
            but one was higher,
            so we slept stairsteps

like drifting-apart rowboats

———

I called it separation

he called it
writing his dissertation in the mountains

———

What do I call you—
Fathers?
You have your secrets too,
but I will never

see you nor
the lines around your eyes,
bitten fingernails, pores
inflamed with drink, or the kindness
that keeps you lingering
wondering
over this questionnaire—

Never see
what he wrote about me—

Well, Fathers,
again it's daddy watching
from the sky
as my high school boyfriend
strokes my thighs
in the warm back seat
of his souped-up Chevy

———

No and again
                    No

—·—

But don't you think
        sometimes God works in us through
                fevered fleshed imagination—

—·—

I used to wish
we would die in 24 hours
and then what would be
the point of silence? What if
I could stand naked
before him, soul-naked,
tinged with fire,
what if I could tell him what would save me?

—·—

        They were out—he said
        Come get your things

Then I stood there in the kitchen

        A voice said, Do it now, die—

—·—

The bride and groom we were
        long ago—if I could
pass my hands before their eyes—
        bring them peace—the tall boy
in the rented tux, the girl with her wings

of hair and the loopy lace
on the white satin bodice—

———

I tear the papers, I have no
answers for you, Fathers

but I have two prayers

———

Make to nothing now the path that led
to the house next to the chicken farm
in Upland, California. And the rocks
and thorns in the chaparral, the yuccas
flourishing their white candles on the mountain
where that man my first husband guided his
black cycle carefully down the winding road—
make them to nothing and my arms around him.
Cancel his birthday lasagnas and cakes,
the salads we ate with our hands
on the porch steps, cancel the ears of corn
we gnawed, slick to the elbows in butter and garlic.
The pomegranates' scarlet star-shaped flowers
outside the window where I lay
suckling my baby son, July so hot
I could barely move—make them of no effect,
erase the pattern of leaves through glass,
the tracery of light and shadow.
To…nothing, neuter, of nullus, none.

And explain that, Fathers,
to the children of this marriage?

———

Make to nothing my self-hatred,
strangler fig, stone, let me
open my hands and let the river
run through them at last, let the cold current
move through me, over me. Cancel
my guilt cancel
his fist through the wall cancel
my children rocking on their beds
the first night I was not there. Cancel
every instant they would vanish
down airport corridors
at the end of school vacations cancel
their airplanes rising let me
magick them back into the sprung night let them
know my love let me
even now cradle them.

As for him let him
die not thinking of me not
hurt by me not
wanting any longer any stray hair
or thumbprint scrap of lace recipe chant
charm or croon that was my passage
through his world. Abolish make nothing
invalidate if that is what he wants.

Let him kneel
with his wife at the altar.

My Dream of the Babies

The babies just *arrived*. There they'd be,
at the top of the stairs. One of them

was Marcia's, but she was in Morocco.

Forlorn little things—no, not exactly—
plump and rosy, just in need of love.

So I'd cuddle them, change them, tuck them in.

The second one—not Marcia's—
pulled a blanket down from the crib rail

to wrap herself warm, and I helped her,

bundled her tight in the handknit yellow blanket,
the sturdy weave with a scalloped edge.

How I loved those babies. Warm. One year old,

and warm. Damp weight in my lap, fuzzy heads
beneath my chin, squirming and twisting

to settle themselves. Then I went somewhere

and forgot a baby. The second one, not Marcia's,
the one who was so agile she could scuttle

up a bureau, then scuttle up a lamp

and sit there laughing. I went somewhere
because this, after all, was my life—

but after several days, *oh my God I left the baby.*

What happened after I hurried back?
In my dream, at least, no catastrophe:

my love for the babies was so strong.

1928. Girl Riding

Gray-eyed girl on the train to Lincoln,
you have folded desire like the dresses
you packed in a steamer trunk, preparing

for freshman year that breathless
August. Freckled girl with small wrists
and a brow lofty and arching, your quiet

gaze vanishes over the autumn fields.
You raise a pastel gold-tipped cigarette
to your lips, and love how the fox collar

of your new brown coat brushes your neck
as you lean against the window;
dreaming, you are delicious to yourself.

No one, not even your sister, has ever
seen your breasts. But you are not thinking
of love, not thinking of college, not thinking

at all as the train carries you deeper
into twilight's beautiful estrangement. If you
get off the train you will become my mother,

so don't, don't, because then I will lose you:
ride forever through the tender night, as smoke
drifts around your carefully drawn lips and soft hair.

Heretic Narrative

So many nights, I hid on my balcony smoking.
Those Berkeley years when you slept downstairs
in that shadowy bedroom, mother, father, how little
I knew of your lives. Once I dropped a cigarette
still lit in the leaves, three stories to the ground,
and panicked—what if I burned us in our beds?—

Pretended I heard a burglar and you, daddy, went outside
and poked around in your pajamas. You had not
died yet. You never knew my jewelry box was full
of butts emptied from car ashtrays
or found in gutters and smoked midnights,
Camels and Pall Malls bearing the kiss
of someone who was not me, her lipsticked freedom—

The city stretching beneath me
as I leaned, thirteen, on the white simple railing
of my balcony. City flowing down the hill
and through the flatlands. Stoplights, streets with cars
and doors open way past bedtime, and music,
bars and coffeehouses and even forbidden
gospel services way down on San Pablo with singing—

Christ, mother and father, what were the carved twin beds about?
I hope you blessed every inch of each other's bodies
because soon you, daddy,
fell to the ground frothing and screaming
with your surprise brain tumor—

Why do we always say Oh you must be careful? You died
so carefully. Those nights the bridge arched across the Bay,
the bridge like diamonds on the pulse
of the beautiful black water, and I read that when people jumped
from the Golden Gate Bridge far over there
between San Francisco and the inkblot headlands,
97% faced the city. I would face the open ocean,
I would once for all face the open ocean—

From the Spirit of the Dead Father

A humming
as if hummingbirds
flew among red flowers among the redwoods

a 42 years' humming

———

Down by the stream where watercress
waved in icy water

We sisters were ordered to go there
cold and bored we squabbled

The camellias
should have been pink
after all that rain they were rotten
and everywhere everyone whispered

When we returned to the room
our mother had already

said goodbye to him

———

I wish you could know me now, father,
wearing my love
It's like a cotton dress
washed   soft
used to be too big for me

J'ai fait la magique étude du bonheur

A shaft of sunlight
slants down through the liquidambar trees,
bronzing the azaleas. At eight I knew,

though none can see God and live,
every dust mote in the light
through the windows of my mother's house

was God. At ten as I got in the tub
I'd carefully lower my foot,
expecting, like Christ, to walk on water.

I was Shadrach, Meshach, Abednego,
who stood with the Lord in fire
and were not consumed.

Sudden Music

—for the boy who spoke only "Animal"
who lived next door to the Mesa Refuge

Our neighbor's rounding up the cows   chuckling   gurgling
their noses and ears loom up, they are born snuffling
out of hill heft
mushi   mushi   poppy and lupine blossoming
sideways
in his eyes for he is tipping his head
calm teeth   sherrr-rip sherrr-rip then ug-ulug-ulug
fat tongue and slobber   phew slurrrip ug-ulug-ulug
the stiff hair selves lumber into his arms
smelling of warm and pee   no hurry

Now our neighbor is shriek and shrike, schreck, he is kit
and white-tailed kite
mrrraow at the cream then a low grating karrrr
then happy, the bright wind hanging him   sweeekrrkrr

Then black things   flints and ants, no sound, our neighbor's
down there somewhere, he's fallen off the world

—Sleep, then—

We are wakened again   swish swuuuush
zeeeeeeeeeeee   whistle   phseeeeeeeeeeeee
now he is rainbird in the marshy fields   fighting
flinging its seedspit

Then he passes to camels and donkeys, it's 4 a.m.
It's the whole shebang, mountain lions and pumas, he's got them
by the balls and they sing from his neck, into his face

22

his heart spurts blood, claws tense, his belly screams
it's the whole feral rodeo

Ayyyyy-up! That's fine, fine, fine, fine, fine, you could say faihn
almost like fan when someone's got you by the throat
kweeeah   hoo   hoo   hoodoo
kweeeah   hoo   hoo   hoodoo
oh he is hawkboy
oh he is great horned owl   all of creation sudden music

What Boat

—for the child who became Sylvie

What boat now brings you out of darkness
into the swoop of barn swallows?
—We say the swallows are rejoicing
because if we could dart and shimmer
and dive and soar as they do, skimming
the air, we would be rejoicing.
As in this noontime thinking of you,
dotterson or *dotterdotter*, I am
rejoicing. You rode in her when she curled
in me, you are big as a berry now
with a beating heart. Grasses blow, heavy
with seed. Queen Anne's lace spreads its snowy
mantles where sunlight warms the wood
that warms my back. This bright and swimming
world will soon be yours. Pollen, thistledown,
hills to the sea in fog below me.
Redwing blackbirds whistling, child.
Sundrunk flies bumbling, buzzing.

Of a Photograph

—Sylvie, three

Look at her
                    dream-filled
one side of her forehead and five cupped fingers
resting against
a display case window. Gazing
at what? Her bones still soft, she presses
the other hand against her mouth
and the fingers bend backward.

White smocked shirt with lollipop flowers,
round tapering eyes, her father's,
her mother's brow
and tangled yellow hair.

All her cells
a riot of growing, her brain
firing, blood coursing, lungs contracting,
expanding—
and she who is sandpiper
firefly always
flicking and darting
from light to shadow and back again,
there is a great silence in her now,
she is spellbound.

Herself with streaks of light
on the other side
of the glass looks back.
Within the reflection of shoulder
and hand
a skull swims forward to meet her—

on a shelf in the case, a human skull,
but hard to see, a trick of the angle—

We were looking at bones
at preschool, she said.
Her hand barely touches the glass.
There's a tiny scratch on her wrist.
Blurred light, wavery imprecision,
herself leaning in
toward herself, and in
and through the image, the nearly
invisible skull.

Look at her.

For Your 100th Birthday

Beloved ash
          beloved nightmare

            Heart-haunter
of the melodious voice

and thin dark bones
          Walk still behind my eyelids

          Rise with the calling owl
as she glides at midnight

Inhabit the silence of berries
          the coyote's scream toward dawn

          Swell in me now
like the ripening figtree

Fill my throat once more
          with the hunt and ache of you

          Last time I saw you
they wheeled you to the fire

And after two years' coma
          what was left to burn

          Implacable mother
Wrecked queen

Family Gatherings

For I will praise my daughters' beautiful haunches.

Sprawled on the couch, draped over each other,
my daughters make a nest and their babies

play between them. It is late afternoon,

in California; light from the stained glass panel
that hangs in the living room window

pours red and gold and green across their hair,

around their shoulders. The thick curve of hips
and thighs, the lines that are just beginning

to come around their mouths and eyes, will linger

in my mind for all the months I do not see them.
And I? Oh body, body. The power that will cast me

like a wad of leaves in the muddy river

is growing in me now. So many years I seemed
unchanging, so many years I ran through life.

Thirty Years After I Left Your Father

—Green Gulch Zen Monastery Gardens

Why should, how could, your bitterness with me
ever completely fade?

We move through fields of lettuce
into quietness between us

toward the shrine with its Buddha,
the enclosure near the sea—

two human creatures
among the trees, nothing but that simple thing.

These mysterious beings called "I,"
and "walk," what is that, a way of moving forward.

No Vow

Calm yourself, here where the blue painted saint
in his wooden shrine
presides over the hillside. The mountain lion
they saw by the barn is not, as you're convinced,
looking especially for you. Yet all you can see
is your own fear, projected on to his twitching tail.

Calm yourself, you who could not fight a dog
or outrun a rattler. There's nothing to be done.
The world makes you no vow.
Flies want what you offer.
Pray all you like, carry a whistle around your neck,
march along the trail singing.
The hay is white and golden in the wind.
The thistles, crowns of thorn, with light on every sepal.

When I Was a Child

Red barrette slicking the hair off my domed
and serious forehead, I turned my blue-lined,
pulpy paper upside down and wrote
left-handed, arm dragging the page, fingers
hooked back toward my chest. With the class
I traced circles and pothooks, struggling to guide
my hand around chaotic scricks and scraws,
to make the shapes that would open the world.

Dismissed for lunch from Shaffer School,
I kicked clumps of ice in gutters or stole
springtime flowers from the neighbors' yards,
wandered home with lilacs and daisies.
"The kitchen" equaled "mother," "Korea"
equaled "father," and in my sister's
history book there rose the world's first
mushroom cloud: luminous, beautiful.

I wanted the world to declare my mother
Mrs. America for her soft breasts, the way
she called me Annie-o, her pretty housedresses
and buffed fingernails. To give my father
Top Top Highest Secret clearance in the Army,
so he could confer with the President,
could be in on things if it came to bombing.
And I wanted to make a shelter
like my friend Wendy's, whose parents

were ready for the Commies, with cans
and bags of cookies stacked on shelves,
cots with Army blankets, toilet paper

and flashlights. At school when we crouched
beneath our desks as the sirens wailed,
I murmured to myself how God
kept his children safe through the fiery furnace.

When I was a child, my world and my words
were at one with my God.
Now my words across the page
move with awkwardness and labor,
because to find You I must write as a beginner.
On the paper's field, some scratches like twigs,
a ragged nest once lined with down,
my letters broken tracks across the snow.

Lullaby

Behind the dream the ocean.

Behind the ocean a tern's egg nested in the sand.

Within the egg a tern riding the waves, sleeping on the waves.

II.

Dream Cabinet

—Fogdö, Sweden

1.

Soft rain. Skies white-gray the same as the water. I lie in the
bottom bunk beneath a green-striped blanket here on Fogdö.
I've wakened from a nightmare, taut with fear.

2.

At the conference in Scotland, Lyn from Haifa said, *Nearly half
my students are Arabs, the other half Israeli.*

*When it gets really bad, I go to the sea and watch the fishing boats.
Nothing has changed in their lives forever.*

3.

>Two days ago, we were still in Scotland—
>*the hottest day in the UK ever.* A columnist
>in the paper wrote of people's hideous fashions:
>
>*Better get used to dressing well when it's hot;*
>*after all, we'll have to cope with worse.*
>
>Cope? We'll choke, gasp, muffled.
>Cry out, the trees are vanishing,
>the blistering heat is rising. We will tip
>
>the planet past the healing point and then—
>Don't they know death wins, and flesh

can be zapped and seared, wars first for oil
then for stolen water, wars for air not just food?
Death will be the kind one, yet so plenteous

are our gizmos there will be no silence, no darkness
even in death. The grave, a brightly lit parking lot—

4.

How to be a muddy field, germy,
                                rank, unseemly?

Here at Fogdö there is beauty.
            Bushes thick with blueberries
                                scatter among boulders.

            But the dream-phrase jumps in my mind:

There's a black pebble lodged against the heart chakra.

5.

                        What do we dream
What do we dream

                Be advised
        I do not exist

            If you are characters in my play
    it does you no harm.

            Daughter, mother, wife—
what am I but passages of light
                        through wave, illuminating
        intransigence,

and bread cupped in a palm,
                    water through hands
         that feel and cherish with the fingertips
                         each slick of leaf, each bent branch

                    as it flows or drifts into infinity—
The rabbits we saw in the field in Scotland
                         hopped off to their nests beneath bushes

as sun hovered toward twilight over the river,
                    the limestone town, hill with distant cattle.

6.

              On the outhouse walls at Fogdö:

              A map of Norrtälje that shows Fogdö
              at the upper edge, facing out to Ålands Hav,
              and, scattered all along, the thousands of islands
              that form the Stockholm Archipelago.

              A print of soldiers called Det ivre or iure
              af ett Soldattalt. Many children's drawings,
              including a Polynesian maiden complete
              with sword, grass skirt, coconut brassière,

              and palm tree. A kangaroo, by Susa.
              Ballerinas, warriors, monsters. A very
              friendly hedgehog. A bright pastel with beach
              umbrella, grapes, a papaya-shaped guitar.

7.

—Sleep, says the sea, sleep, says the sea, the birds
thicken in the trees as light glints across the water.

A breeze. Late afternoon, the light growing pewter,
soft Falun red of the ramshackle summer house

soaking up shadows. Out on the water, a motorboat.
I would like to spend the curve of a year

from bird cherries to mushrooms, svamp, in Sweden.
Trace the circle round through lilacs, king's-blood-lilies,

lilies of the valley, then blueberries, strawberries,
raspberries, then lingonberries, apples.

To gather them as they ripen, wander along
with that rapt purposeful emptiness, every sense alert

for a glimpse of red or blue, the scrotal sponginess
of puffballs, luminescence of chanterelles.

To know this place in the fullness of its seasons.
And watch the light on water, day after day,

empty out my everlasting self-regard.
Let the sunlight, fog, or rain have its will with me.

8.

> At Fogdö, I thought, the silence of myself
> would come back to me. But the children cry
> as evening comes, and love's no easier
> here where blueberries ripen on shin-high
> bushes and wild strawberries nestle, sparse,
> in the roadside ditches. Love's no easier
> for Frida, our hostess, her new lover's absent,
> she grows thinner every day. She tells us,
> *Here you may take coffee, and here,*
> *on this bench, you may sit for romance.*

9.

Can't you stay awake one night
to watch the sky that never turns black

grow light again? Can't you stay
awake one night to hear the soft rain?

10.

Where I live they are paving the world.
The oaks they're saving perish,
hemmed in by concrete. Dogwoods parch
and wither in a season of no rain. You'd think
we'd think of the collapse of systems—
at a certain point, technology cannot save us.
Earth sickens and sickens, and finally
turns mean. Only things with thorns survive.

11.

I'm reading Kandinsky, he speaks about green
as the resting point between yellow and blue,

the color of tranquility and regeneration.
Surrounded by trees and water, I want

to be writing of peace, want to be moving into that deeper
harmony where earth and sea and sky seep into, into,

every pulse of my blood. But I keep thinking
to write of peace right now is to be a tourist.

12.

Here, at eight, when the children go to sleep,
it's still soft daylight. Gulls are crying over the inlet.

And now they stop. It's absolutely silent—so silent
I can hear the spiders crawl across the page,
and each drop of pee falling in the outhouse bucket.

Yes, this is now, it's not escape and not evasion:
the just-so of water, light, and silence.

13.

Now the lip, lip, lip of the quiet water between the islands.

How to paint water?—the tiny ripples flowing
from right to left—and the islands

stretching away, each with its own tranquility.

To live here all the seasons, be of this place,
like the sea captain buried in the graveyard:

what battening down would it take, to survive its winters?

In the distance, light catches a couple of tiny buildings,
and smoke rises, or is it a plume of clouds,

far on the horizon. Little color in this scene—pearly gray,
charcoal gray, swan's-down, pine green; all twilit—

On the water, an orange float partly hidden by grasses.

14.

Kind summer, facing west as sun goes down.
The ducks still bob about the water, the Baltic opens up

between the islands, and the body grows calm
in its own contingencies. On the pier at Fogdö

a woman sits—a woman who is I—
and the sun shatters in a path across the water.

The ducks drift to and fro, and a few birds
honk and chirp, shriek and coo.

One motorboat's revving back toward a hidden cove.
A spiderweb stretches like a line of laundry

from a rock to the pier, catches the slant of diminishing daylight.
Now the ducks are swimming home,

the little ones in front of their elders. Flies buzz my head.
Frida has just come out to wash Logan's bottle.

Amazing, to trust the world so much
you'll wash your baby's bottle in the ocean—

Now Julia, five, is singing somewhere outside.
La la la la la   la   la la la la la la.

And Logan, two, says goodbye to every rock in the ocean.
One by one he tosses pebbles in,
chants *Bye bye weewee, bye bye weewee.*

15.

Be free. In Swedish, *Var frei.* Prospero
says, I will not marshal you any longer.
        And at the same time
               drowns his book

those loops and scrolls
      those cross-hatchings and bent sticks
clumsily woven baskets that hold meaning
            releases them

they unweave they unloop

        see the pages
     bits of print bits of cursive
           still visible

rise like Ariel (rise like April)

      And now Prospero grows old, is silent

and now all around us the white looping air.

16.

          You're not coming, are you,
    god of ferocity and exaltation? You're waiting
    up there near the high mountain passes,

    where the ravens wheel up against the sun,
    and the tight green pinecones ripen like roses.
    You're waiting and then you'll fall upon

some unsuspecting traveler, leap on his back
and ride him down. Here, the flat sea,
where the water ripples luminous

with the patina of old pewter. This calm
that has no words, the day spinning slowly
off its spool, and all night long the light not gone.

17.

I'm sitting on the pier as my husband sleeps beside me.
It's water nearly all the way around,
rippling with striations of shadow and light.

The ducks are floating ahead of me, growing near
the forested island. The birds are crying their long good-nights.
Like being inside a pearl: the perfect roundness of the summer evening.

Water—slate blue, gray-blue, with midges dancing on it.
Now the ducks are sailing away from me.
The sun's still white, but sinking toward the horizon.

Now the sun's a fish, caught in the Baltic seagrasses.
My husband's sleeping peacefully, his whole face soft. Sometimes
I can't help touching him even though I know it will wake him.

18.

A single bird perches on a branch—a wren, a willow branch.

When the doors of the dream cabinet open, the bird flies away...
into our lives.

And the branch remains, to carry its singing.

III.

BP

1.

Serious harm or damage to life

                                    Dear Sirs:

    (including fish and other
aquatic life), to property,   **Dragonflies**
to any mineral deposits (in areas   **hover**
leased or   **catching the light**
                  emerald, turquoise, ruby, translucent

not leased), to the national security

                     Born of water
      or defense   **they sport with land**
                  but lay their eggs in water

or to the marine, coastal, or human environments;

                   where oil clogs the membrane
     blowouts, fires, spillages, or   **of their**
other major accidents . . .   **wings**

                Above the slick among the grasses
                    one dragonfly scrubs
              its oiled face
       a threat of harm
       or damage to life . . .
             filthy
                  iridescence
to take affirmative action to abate

the violation

2.

The pelicans spread their feathers
            spiky and stiff with gunk   Now that we are beyond the oil-covered-
                                    birds phase, establishing definitive
                            links between the spill and whatever biogenetic
                            or ecological disturbances are in store is
strain forward above the slick but   only going to get harder. . . .
            cannot rise
                            Graveyards of recently deceased coral,
      gape, flap   oiled crab larvae, evidence of bizarre
squeak and bark, squawk
            flail   sickness in the phytoplankton and bacterial
                            communities, and a mysterious brown

      amid sea oats
viscous water
                            liquid coating large swaths of the ocean
                      floor, snuffing out life underneath. . . .
                                  consequences as severe as
                      commercial
Contaminated
      inside and out
the pelicans mottled
            with poison
                      fishery collapses and even species
                                  extinction—

3.

"I have not been there, I have not seen it.
It means little to me, a matter of blogs and soundbytes.
Not ordering oysters at the oyster bar."

            Flames roll over the waters,
            lick the legs of our chairs
            where we sit sipping coffee.

Sweetgum Country

Billy shows us his arm, burned by the sun
where pesticides sensitized his skin
those years of his childhood, playing
in Delta cotton fields. A charred,
hand-sized lozenge marks the tender crease
inside his elbow. Alex holds up her chart
that shows the sickness and death
in her mother's family, from cancer
in Cancer Alley. She has made red circles
for "fought," green crosses for "died,"
she has put stars around her name,
my pretty dark-haired student.
They come to class, my sixteen freshmen,
and no matter what their topics,
they all say, "I never *knew* this..."

Fords and Chevies that will barely crank
one more time are parked in the reeds
and slick red mud. Early evening sun
pours down on the cypresses and sweetgum,
the Tallahatchie swamp at the edge
of Marshall County. Turtles poke their heads up.
Cottonmouths zipper through black water
or stretch out long and bask on the abandoned
railroad bridge. Men and women of all ages
beguile the hours after work,
the idle hours, with soft talk or silence,
with bamboo poles and battered coolers.
They could use the food.
They fish for buffalo, catfish, bass,
despite the fish advisories, the waters laced with mercury.

Army Men

1.

Isaac, for whom I prayed, is back from Iraq.
My poetry student three years ago, before he left
he said, *I joined ROTC for the scholarship,*
why else? The Marines made me a pacifist.

He's different now, when we have lunch.
One eyelid twitches, small as a waterbug's
ripples on still water. *They're crazy,*
they love to kill each other. . . He picks up his spoon,

lifts soup but doesn't eat. *We slept on the ground,*
didn't wash . . . we drove around, filled in
wherever they needed us. He's jumpy,
starts to eat but lets the spoon drop.

When Katrina hit I got my 100-gallon
water jug and drove on down to the coast.
We lost it all but I was home
in the wreckage and death and nothing.

Just like Iraq, it was great . . .
The muscles of his face tighten.
I'm not a pacifist anymore.
I've done things that I'm ashamed of.

2.

You do what you gotta do, he says.
I'd like to say I don't understand him but I do.

When I was small, my Army father showed me
how to kill a man:

surprise him from behind,
wrap your arm around his neck,
and then *Crack!* he'd pretend to do it to me,
yank up on the jaw, and *There goes the neck bone.*

For years I dreamed my father
lurking through darkness with his billy club,
sneaking up behind, then *crack!* to bad Koreans.
Or hacking at jungles, guarding prisoners.

Or kidnaped in a Quonset hut, chained
and tortured for secrets, with only a bowl
and a concrete floor. I was sure
they would find a twin for my father

and send him to Japan to join us.
My mother would be fooled, accept his gifts
of garnets and pearls, never know
he was locked up somewhere.

3.

My father never talked about his wars.
I never saw on his face that tight
jumpy snarl with which Isaac seems to gaze
into brutal efficiency, into screaming.

But my mother said, when she picked him up
at the Omaha train station, Christmas '45,
she found him alone on a bench
at the far end of the room, huddled over,

head in his hands. When I asked her what was wrong
she said, *If you don't know I can't tell you.*
And she said it took months for the telegram to reach her,
the telegram he sent to let her know he was returning,

because he addressed it simply: *Home Street.*

4.

What do I know of my father? Not much.

As a child, I leapt to my feet
whenever I heard "The Star-Spangled Banner,"
climbed from the car to stand at attention
at "Taps" while they folded the flag.

In the basement in the '50's, Pennsylvania,
my father kept his billyclub. Somewhere,
his rifles and pistols. In his bureau,
the dogtags, the medals for marksmanship.

He wrote us stories about a dog named Pinkelfritz
and a dog named Fritzpinkel
and a cat named Kitty Blue Ribbon, from Seoul.
He shined his shoes every Sunday morning.

At the end of World War II
he screamed, once, in his honeymoon sleep.
But my mother told me that. She also said,

on the road to Manila
he could smell the bodies burning.

Three for Mr. Keys

1. *1970. Emmett Till*

In suits and two-tone heels, the mothers
lined up at the back of the classroom
to supervise. Outside the international
school, barges heaped with coal
labored up and down the Meuse
in Belgium past slag heaps, pollard sycamores,
slick wet roads, clod-gummed fields,
towns built of slate. And the students

who had never heard "a Negro"
listened to Mr. Keys
as he told them the history of civil rights.
An hour a day for a week they bent
their shining heads over pencils
as the guest speaker from back home
talked to them in his voice that rolled
like a river. And the mothers hovered, anxious

lest he tell what they called a biased story—
Mr. Keys, principal of a one-room school
in southern Mississippi, who couldn't keep his job
if he didn't get a Master's, and couldn't
get a Master's in southern Mississippi,
so the man whose life he'd saved
at the Battle of the Bulge
helped him get a Master's in Liège—

Tonight I entered my hometown public library.
A boy in a special exhibit,
big as life, shot in black and white,
strode grinning toward me.

No one had hurt him yet, this boy
Mr. Keys told us about in the final hour.
His flesh as warm, as radiant,
as the flesh of those long-ago seventh graders.

2.   *Mr. Keys*

The night of my party to celebrate
the triumph of our school's experimental
Civil Rights Week—because even the mothers
agreed that Mr. Keys "had handled himself
with dignity"— I cooked tacos
for thirty-five students and turned the volume
floor-shaking loud on "She Loves You"
so the kids could jump around in our
seventh-floor apartment that looked down
on the star-shaped flowerbed.

When I went up to Mr. Keys silent on the couch
and tried to coax him to his feet,
what I learned was that he didn't
want to dance with me. But I was his hostess,
in my flowing hippie dress, and I begged him
"Don't be shy," so he steered me
till the end of the song
like a chunk of wood through a tiny box-step.

Now I consider his home, where to put
his hands on *the white girl* could mean death.

3. *Then, April*

In his brown cardigan and father shoes
he sat in the parlor of his friend's house,
looking out over fields spiked with green
beneath a Flemish sky. His friend,
a quiet Belgian, gave us coffee.
The light grew pale and a chill came
to the early evening. Mr. Keys had got his Master's.

He would go back to the peeling
beadboard building where the water faucets
leaked rust and half the books
bore some other school's DISCARD stamps.

Back when I was young, I thought
he would be happy. Wanted him
to be sad at saying good-bye to me.

Wanted him to give me something
I could keep. But he just
looked up from his coffee, said, "I'm tired."

The Getting-Lost Drive

Last night we slammed doors till the paint chipped.
Today I'm sucked dry as an old bone.
But even in misery, this white-haired,
sunburnt man, who glowers through beetling
eyebrows and stomps around the house,
this man and I are wedded at the marrow.
So we take a vow to drive in silence.
In the car we turn left   right   left   by hunch,
down the darker roads, toward the higher trees.
Away, away from everything we know,
trying to get lost, hoping something will surprise us.

Headed home, outside Holly Springs,
we pass the bait shop with its live crickets
and iridescent plastic crawlers,
where our five kids once stood rapt
before the display of gold-dazzler feely things
and notched red or green ones,
finally making their choices which five
sparkly creatures they could buy for a dollar
and line up on the dashboard, where the lures
would shimmer and soften in the sun
on our long-ago happier get-lost drives—

And we pass a black Lab, mostly bones,
that plods through sun-scorched clover.

              No matter where you go—
along the gravel logging roads, outside
the rusted trailers, toward Water Valley, Tula,

Coontown Landing, Wyatt Crossing—
you see unwanted, unloved dogs.
Nobody misses them, no child wakes
to mourn them, secretly leaves water
hoping they'll return. These ditch-spawn,
failed hunting dogs, abandoned in the pine-woods—
I don't know what their longing finds them.
Alone or shuffling in packs,
past howling, nearly past hunger,
they keep walking, it's summer,
their tongues swell, their feet burn.

La Garde Guérin

—traveling with friends in the south of France

The first few days, the facts enchant me:
Three feet thick, the walls of this hotel

kept enemies at bay, for the knights called *pariers*
built strong, banding together for peace

and promising safe passage to the *jongleurs,*
*marchands, pelerin*s—three great types

of medieval travelers. Once, the village thrived
with the ancient occupations—cartmaker,

dairy worker, pig butcher, wool spinner.
Plowman with horses, plowman with oxen.

Wood chopper, farrier, keeper of rabbits.
But the peasants left the hard life of the mountains.

Now the tourists come, it's *Un Grand Village.*
And we come too, with hiking boots and daypacks,

to taste the chestnut honey, climb the local footpaths.
Our children grown, we think that all back home

is well. Each night we drink *un verre*
among the red geraniums

where swallows dart and swoop among the shadows.

Sunlight passes from one tawny window
to the other, to the right and left of this stone altar,

lighting up the floor in quiet circles—
it is poor, this Romanesque chapel, its narrow

leaded windows set in granite
that has weathered for a thousand years.

Since the moment the phone call came from home,
fear has pulled me back to light more votives,

more votives, place them in the bank of votives—
I have become any woman, any century, lighting candles for her son—

But one night I leave the village on the rock and heather path
toward Le Mont, and double over suddenly

screaming and wailing beneath the faint stars, to know
how many have begged to God to help the children they loved,

and the heavens answered nothing, and still this suffering continues—

———

Someone approaches behind me on the pitch-black trail,
wraps strong arms around me and won't let go.

I do not even know whose arms they are—my husband's?
Our friend's? His French wife's? —Yes, she who knows me least

knows what to do. She hangs on and rocks me,
glues herself to my back. Her arms like those *parier* walls enclose me.

He's young, she says, *he's young… he'll work his journey out….*

Dry October

All day, every day, Carl sits on his front porch
in a sprung red armchair. Emaciated, gray,
he cradles beer as his radio numbs time

with spiky music, muffled voices, rising laughter.
My son says, *he's trying to kill himself.*
Once we brought him home when he was draped

around a light pole. He kept mumbling thanks—
last thing I need is for the cops to write me up.
Once he told us, he trained to be a Jesuit—

*then I joined the navy, came home to sell cheap furniture
and nurse my ailing Momma.* He's a sweet man,
Carl—married, divorced, married, divorced—

Grass wilts in my driveway, and tufts of tiny flowers,
tough roots clutching the cracked macadam.
Sometimes when I'm sweeping there, he and I call hi.

The scarlet vincas blanch and crumple.
Bamboo runners snake across the ground
and bamboo shoots fight up through parched wisteria.

No rain for months. The redbuds are losing their leaves.
Tat tvam asi, the Upanishads preach: *That art thou.*
The soul, the All, are one.

In my hedge, a tangle of thorns entwines
with the red-orange leaves of Carolina creeper.
Above Carl's radio, mockingbirds call.

In this dry October a strange peace rises.

Teaching Yoga in the Kali Yuga

If You come to get us, Lord,
we will be open wide in Triangle.
Tornado sirens wail and lightning

jabs through trees outside, stabs heaven
to earth, all light sucked from the late
afternoon as the storm comes snarling.

Nine of us, our mats arranged like a star
in this renovated train station
in Oxford, Mississippi, where we practice

yoga. Yoga from Yuj: union. Where's to run,
where's safety when You smack trees
to trash, pluck children like wildflowers

only to drop them miles away, broken
in mud-choked ditches? We are bending
over now, *knees straight,* I say, *one hand*

on each side of the forward foot, let your
body flow over the leg, breathe, release.
The sky screams, trees whip and thrash

and splinter, we come out of the pose
to shut the big wood double doors.
Because I'm the teacher I can't surrender

to terror, though terror
would take me, quenchless, bones lights liver
and all, if this circle were broken.

If You come to get us, Lord, we will be
standing now in Mountain. When the tornado
passes near, it roars just like a train.

Now we are lying in Corpse, *eyes closed,* I say,
arms and legs apart, hands cupping open
to the skies. Let your breath rise deep and full,

rise like a wave, like light, filling you and joining you
with everything that is. Let it flow
in and out across the threshold of your body.

Rain Stick

I have watched you,
first in the sunny room in Charlottesville
as you were learning Yeats's "Long-Legged Fly,"

and I have lain beside you as you stilled
to remember just how a line turned, the actual adjective.
I've touched your hip as you said me "Tintern Abbey"

or Hardy's "Afterwards," in the dark I've felt that joy,
seen that hedgehog, those white moths.
When I sprained my knee, trying to learn to ski,

I tossed in the bottom bunk of our hut
as your voice at three a.m. floated down above me,
murmuring "Fern Hill," the horses "walking warm

out of the whinnying green stable,"
because I begged you, "Tell me something beautiful."
I slept on our wedding night

as you drove for hours through the Blue Ridge Mountains,
waked and slept again, hypnotized by your tenderness
as you said me the whole Rubaiyat—

one of the thousand poems you know by heart.
For more than twenty years,
I have heard your husky voice reciting poetry.

We were talking on the phone, I in California,
you back home in Mississippi.
You said, "The poems we love are vanishing."

I had nothing to reply. Then after some moments
you brought the rain stick to the phone,
the gourd we bought at a concert long ago,

when Robin Williamson played thirty-five instruments—the
lute, the rebeck, the psaltery, and the harp—
and sang and recited Bardic tales and mysteries.

You tipped the gourd so I could hear
the hidden seeds running down its length,
still making the sound of rain.

If Not, Winter—

A squirrel leaps the air between pecan trees,
lands upside down thirty feet high,
then scrabbles along a shimmying branch

to safety. And small invisible birds
trill *here, here, here*
in the willow oak, magnolia,

here now in the privet, as I lie flat on my porch
with my face receiving sun,
the shadows long across the grass.

For the first time since surgery
I have opened up my brace.
I have propped my betadine-yellow leg

and wrapped my swollen foot in cabbage leaves.
I lie here, simply breathing,
old wood of this old house holding me,

Christmas lights left all year
looping and shining along the wistaria vine,
through the porch's hand-carved cornices.

Praise for the glacial knit of bone,
ebb of lymph, gradual shrinking of elephant skin.
For my husband who has walked along behind me,

holding to my waist as I wobbled on my crutches,
then slid my pants down,
stretched out my hurt leg as I hovered

toward the toilet. And my son who made us pizza.
For, winter over, forsythia nearly in leaf.
For these bandages stuck to my knee,

the black slug tracks of blood, steel pins
holding my bones together. For the moments
that fling me down. And the seasons that slowly heal me.

Lay

Ah, your hot throat on my mouth.
Close your eyes, let me ruin you, love.
The willow oak at twilight
outside our open window
swings cool and black to the clouds
and spring peepers sing to the rain.

All in green I lay you down
where light surprises the cedars,
where wet earth claims and soothes
your stung flesh. This music
ripples like minnows.
All in green I take you riding.

The dogs of belief lie down
here, where curve and urge say
now, where your importunate eyes
summon sharp, summon sweet
out of me. Not hard to say *forever*.
Your hot throat. Our dominions.

Cicadas, Summer

And the night continues relentlessly,
gathering its creatures. Beneath the trees,
in the heat-wrung leaves, cicadas throb
and stir up time to a crescendo. Try to sleep.
Every twitching muscle plagues you, every
troubled thought comes home, you rustle
and shift in the sodden rumple of one o'clock,
two o'clock, three o'clock. Loth to touch flesh,
you sprawl on the bed as heat bears down
and oozes you, as tree frogs chirp
with a small incessant music. Loosen
the doors of the sense. The Mississippi
summer holds you, outlaw and believer.

———•———

I remember the river of roaches
that flowed from the gutter into the old
Jitney Food Center, and back again, like
boatmen from hell, that night we walked
across town to have another look
at the old house we were choosing to buy—
remember stepping over them
twenty years ago in the soupy night.
Before the heat broke I fought with my husband.
Afterwards as he lay asleep
with not enough hours until morning,
I was swept with such tenderness for him.
The wild pink climbing roses were in bloom,
tangled through the trees, and cicadas
in the branches whirred up to carry me.

Cassandra

—Useless Bay on Whidbey Island

The tide comes up around the driftwood palaces
and spreads across the dirty sand like satin.
Windows across the bay catch fire from the setting sun.

Long ago I wanted to play Cassandra—
marked for death, my face ablaze,
to stand center stage, declaiming

as the Furies, the Mothers,
began to swarm and buzz pitiless, incessant,
though no one but I could hear them, see them.

To know what would happen,
must happen—
yet turn from the sunlight to enter the house.

Then turn once again, at the threshold,
arms flung out,
and cry *Sun! I see you for the last time!*

———

The owl hunts blood among the fir trees,
and when I sleep I hear
                    torn shadow.

All night, alone in this island cabin,
I guard her in my dream—
my child, wild daughter: the knives, the cries, not yet come near.

Credo

But the cardinal, the birdsong, do not need you,
to pulse forward into the light. The peaches do not need you,

to swell and soften, dark with the sugars of summer.
Oh you can be the flesh their juices run down,
but you do not make the seed nor the earth it grows in.

And the artist, what is she? The one whose hands are empty.
Who says—though to what, I do not know—
speak through me as you will.
Who calls the made thing out of the sheltering darkness.

                  Now the day is full of leaves.
After the rain, the sky is low and white as ash.
The ragged garden spikes and trembles.

Thirty Years

For Peter

—What if I hadn't got a babysitter,
hadn't put on my silky
fawn-colored blouse and flowered cotton

1980's skirt and gone to that party
where you stood in your gray pinstripe suit
in the department chairman's garden?

—you speaking intensely with some colleague,
and when I asked if you liked teaching
at Virginia you said "No." What if

you hadn't said "No," which stunned
my desperate affability? And if
you hadn't caught when I leapt?

What a liar I'd become: good mother,
lousy wife, groomed for "success"
in my business suits. We botched that,

sweetheart, didn't we? —When we stood
beneath a tree outside that courthouse,
me clutching a ring too big for my finger,

you wearing that same gray suit again,
our children in their party clothes
holding their little bouquets,

and the Sheriff of Albemarle County
asked the Lord to keep us, I promised myself
I would be your wife forever.

Tonight, I miss you.
I'm listening to Jan Garbarek
improvise on sax. I'll be home soon.

Over All a Mist of Sweetness

I cannot gather them all, the thousands
and thousands of berries
these warm September days
keep pushing forward. Behind every
glossy, nubbly sugar-tip at the end
of every branch, the little ones
line up, still green, awaiting their turn
to ripen in what has become
the diminishing summer. And of these
trailing thorny branches, some in forest shadow
are still decked out with faintest
lilac blossoms. I wander from bush
to bush in a mania of abundance.
Every afternoon I lean my body
gingerly against the prickles,
plastic bucket in my left hand,
my right hand snaked around,
between, reaching for just that perfect one,
the fat one thrust up behind the spiderweb,
or there, that cluster, hanging black
with juice against a cloudless sky.
So thick are the berries, when I
look back across the grassy field
and squint against the sun,
the landscape's smudged, inky. Yes I know
others have written of blackberries,
but these are *my* fingers gently twisting
the tender, knobbly fruit from the hull,
this is *my* hour and cherishing, I breathe
blackberry into every cell of my body.
Bees love me. They come to buzz

and hover around my crimson fingers.
In this stained, thorn-pricked
meditation, nothing needs
to happen. Then the chittering of a bird,
reeds slowly rustling in a sudden, fitful breeze.
The barred owl lifts heavy
from a nearby fir,
a yellow beech leaf drifts downward.

It Was Snowing and It Was Going to Snow

Unseasonal weird once in a green moon Mississippi beauty—
deep deep snow. We woke early, dressed,
walked through the silent town and Bailey's Woods
to Faulkner's house, before anyone but a deer
had made prints, we trudged through abundance.
I held my husband's arm down the uneven trail,
the snow-mound stairs of the woods,
because I was afraid to fall, knowing how suddenly
bones break. Again and again when I touch him
I am filled with joy for the sheer fact of him
among all the infinite spaces—this burly,
beetle-browed man with the muscular legs
and fine-pored skin. Now, through my window,
grays and taupes of gingko and maple,
fractals of branches softened and warmed with snow,
then the greens of privets massed shabby beyond them,
and way down the hill, the Methodist Church
just barely red, a smudge through the trees. Someone
has built a snowman, someone is romping with a dog.
Soon night will climb the hill outside the window
where I wait for the white bees to swarm,
surrounding the branches, the house,
surrounding my sleep, scattering their cold pollen again.

Notes

Heretic Narrative

"Heretic narrative" is a phrase from the chapter "The Long Vacation" in Charlotte Brontë's novel *Villette*; Lucy Snowe uses it to describe her rebellious life story.

From the Spirit of the Dead Father

Tome Adzievski's sculpture "Spirit of a Dead Father" (1996) is part of the Djerassi Residency's sculpture collection, in Woodside, California.

Sudden Music

Several years ago I had a residency at Mesa Refuge in Point Reyes, California. Next door lived a boy who did not speak human language; he spoke *animal*. We never saw him but we heard him.

"J'ai fait la magique étude du bonheur"

From Arthur Rimbaud's poem "O saisons, ô châteaux," this translates as "I have made the magical study of happiness."

What Boat

"Dotterson" and "dotterdotter" are Swedish for grandson and granddaughter.

BP

Quoted phrases in Part 1 are from the National Commission on the BP Deepwater Horizon Oil Spill and Offshore Drilling January 2011 Report to the President. Quoted phrases in Part 2 are from Naomi Klein, "After the Spill," *The Nation*, January 31,

2011. The italicized lines at the end of the poem are from our anonymous, collective response.

Teaching Yoga in the Kali Yuga

According to traditional Hindu cosmology, we are now nearing the end of the Kali Yuga (the Age of Iron), the final and most negative of four evolutionary Yugic cycles. It is a time characterized by violence, opposition, greed, discord, and materialism.

If Not, Winter—

The title of this poem is unabashedly the same as the title of Anne Carson's translation of Sappho.

Cassandra

This is the way I remember the line, but I have not found it again; the impulse is Cassandra's, but whether it is expressed in just these words, I do not know.

Over All a Mist of Sweetness

The title is taken from the Bardic legend "The Voyage of Bran, Son of Febal," performed by Robin Williamson.

Publication Credits

My warm thanks to the editors of the following journals and anthologies, in which these poems appeared or will appear, sometimes in different versions:

"Family Gatherings" and "It Was Snowing and It Was Going to Snow" — *Adanna*

"J'ai fait la magique étude du bonheur" — *Blackbird*

"Lullaby" — *Bombay Gin*

"If Not, Winter—" and "When I Was a Child" — *Copper Nickel*

"The Getting-Lost Drive" — *Cutthroat*

"From the Spirit of the Dead Father" — *Ekphrasis*

"Dream Cabinet" — *HOW2*; reprinted in *Rampike*

"BP" — *Interim Magazine*

"Heretic Narrative" — *Natural Bridge*

"Army Men" — *Nightsun*; reprinted in *Babel Fruit*

"Cicadas, Summer" and "Disorder and Early Sorrow" — *Oranges & Sardines*

"Lay" — *Oxford American*

"La Garde Guérin," "Slow Rain, October" (as "Rain. October"), "Thirty Years After I Left Your Father" — *Poemeleon*

"1928. Girl Riding" — *Poetry International*

"Answers I Did Not Give to the Annulment Questionnaire" (as "Answers She Did Not Give…") — *Poetry Kanto*

"What Boat" — *Poetry Kanto;* reprinted in *Grand: The Magazine for Grandparents*

"No Vow" and "Sudden Music" — *The Southeast Review*

"Of a Photograph" — *The Squaw Valley Review 2009*

"Sweetgum Country" — *The Valparaiso Review;* reprinted in *Canary*

"Army Men" and "Three for Mr. Keys" were published in *The Southern Poetry Anthology*, Volume II: Mississippi, ed. Steve Gardner and William Wright, Texas Review Press, 2009.

"Rain Stick" was published in *When She Named Fire,* ed. Andrea Hollander Budy, Autumn House Press, 2008.

"Slow Rain, October" was published in *Visiting Doctor Williams: Poems Inspired by the Life and Work of William Carlos Williams,* ed. Thom Tammarro, University of Iowa Press, 2011.

"Dream Cabinet" was featured in the ecopoetry exhibition "Skylines," curated by Elizabeth-Jane Burnett, at the Centre for Contemporary Art and the Natural World, Haldon Forest Park, Exeter, UK, Spring/Summer 2009. "Dream Cabinet" was a finalist in the 2006 Center for Book Arts Chapbook Competition and was runner-up in the 2006 *Missouri Review* Editors' Choice Poetry Awards. It was also a finalist in the 2009 Slash Pine Chapbook Competition and the 2010 *qarrtsiluni* Chapbook Competition. Section 7 of "Dream Cabinet" is published in *qarrtsiluni.*

"From the Spirit of the Dead Father" received a Pushcart nomination. "Three for Mr. Keys" was a finalist in the 2008 Joy Harjo Poetry Competition, *Cuthroat.* "When I Was a Child" was a finalist in the 2010 *Copper Nickel* Poetry Competition.

"Over All a Mist of Sweetness" will appear as a broadside created by Hedgebrook.

Acknowledgments

Warm thanks to Chana Bloch, Alicia Casey, Chrissy Davis, Sharon Dolin, Beth Ann Fennelly, Chris Hayes, Hilda Raz, Corinna McClanahan Schroeder, Danielle Sellers, Gary Short, Peter Wirth, and the members of my online workshop. Also to The Mesa Refuge, the Djerassi Resident Artists Program, the Nebraska Summer Writers' Workshop, and Hedgebrook, for residencies during which some of these poems were written; and to the University of Mississippi's English Department and College of Liberal Arts, for grants.

Many thanks to my editor, Bryce Milligan, for his support of my work once again.

Above all, my love and thanks to four generations of my family—parents, husband, children, grandchildren—just for being themselves.

About the Author

Ann Fisher-Wirth is the author of *Blue Window*, *Five Terraces* and *Carta Marina: A Poem in Three Parts* and the chapbooks *The Trinket Poems*, *Walking Wu Wei's Scroll* and *Slide Shows*. She has received a *Malahat Review* Long Poem Prize, the Rita Dove Poetry Award, the Mississippi Institute of Arts and Letters Poetry Award, and two Mississippi Arts Commission Poetry Fellowships. She has received eleven Pushcart nominations and a 2007 Pushcart Special Mention.

Fisher-Wirth has held Fulbrights to Switzerland and Sweden. She teaches at the University of Mississippi, and teaches yoga at Southern Star Yoga and Blue Laurel Yoga, both in Oxford.

Wings Press was founded in 1975 by Joanie Whitebird and Joseph F. Lomax, both deceased, as "an informal association of artists and cultural mythologists dedicated to the preservation of the literature of the nation of Texas." Publisher, editor and designer since 1995, Bryce Milligan is honored to carry on and expand that mission to include the finest in American writing—meaning all of the Americas, without commercial considerations clouding the choice to publish or not to publish.

Wings Press attempts to produce multicultural books, ebooks, chapbooks, CDs, and broadsides that, we hope, enlighten the human spirit and enliven the mind. Everyone ever associated with Wings has been or is a writer, and we know well that writing is a transformational art form capable of changing the world, primarily by allowing us to glimpse something of each other's souls. Good writing is innovative, insightful, and interesting. But most of all it is honest.

Likewise, Wings Press is committed to treating the planet itself as a partner. Thus the press uses as much recycled material as possible, from the paper on which the books are printed to the boxes in which they are shipped.

As Robert Dana wrote in *Against the Grain*, "Small press publishing is personal publishing. In essence, it's a matter of personal vision, personal taste and courage, and personal friendships." Welcome to our world.

Colophon

This first edition of *Dream Cabinet*, by Ann
Fisher-Wirth, has been printed on 55 pound
EB Natural paper in Ann Arbor, Michigan.
Titles have been set in Aquiline Two and Adobe
Caslon type, the text in Adobe Caslon type. All
Wings Press books are designed and pro-
duced by Bryce Milligan.

On-line catalogue and ordering:
www.wingspress.com

Wings Press titles are distributed
to the trade by the
Independent Publishers Group
www.ipgbook.com
and in Europe by
www.gazellebookservices.co.uk

Also available as an ebook.